A Little Blood, A Little Rain

Mary Carroll-Hackett

FUTURECYCLE PRESS
www.futurecycle.org

Library of Congress Control Number: 2016936228

Copyright © 2016 Mary Carroll-Hackett
All Rights Reserved

Published by FutureCycle Press
Lexington, Kentucky, USA

ISBN 978-1-942371-03-8

For my beautiful sister Andrea Hoyle Goodwin,
my Crickett,
for always being there,
for being a light and a rock and a friend,
no matter what fell—blood or rain.

Contents

Alice Learns to Start Something 9
The Collecting of Fragile Things 10
A Poor Girl's History, and Doc Martens 11
A Little Blood, A Little Rain 12
Shampagne 13
Some Mornings Are Chronic 14
Rilke's Sister 15
Any Room Is a Panic Room 16
He Wants to Know Why I Move So Fast 17
The Name Itself 18
I Am Fish and Salt 19
There Is Someone Asking Not to Be Kissed 20
The Uncleanness of Women 21
It Is Not What Waits At the Door, This Love 22
I Will Not Cut Off My Toes for You 23
Someone Said Once We Are All Deviled 24
Deer, Inarticulated 25
For Dawn and a Dollar 26
Instead of Prayer 27
Love Is a Ferris Wheel 28
Blood Feud in a Place Called Sometime 29
Waking Up at the End of the Day 30
When the Bears Were Starving in Virginia 31
In Preparation for an Elegy 32
Winter Is a Wing-Ache 34
I Will Be Your Country Soon 35
When Angels Come in Earthquakes 36
While Searching This Morning Through Poems About Longing 37
My Hips Roll Like Clay 38
Trailer Park Oracle 39
Hope Is a Folding Chair 40
From the Bones of Flowers 42
200 Miles from Baltimore 43
Twice a Day, the Tide Erases 44

What I Will Give You, If You Will Let Me 45
How to Fry Catfish 46
The Universe in Three Acts: Please Refer to Your Handout 47
A Chant Against Lonely 48
If I Am to Die by Fire 49
Signs of Winter Mammals 50
Last Night I Prayed for Rain 52
You Need to Know Something Else About This Softness 53
The Language of Ice 54
On the Darkening Green 55
Instead of Wings 56
Not the Bloom 57
Praise This and That 58
Notions of the Body 60
Grace Where You Find It 62

Alice Learns to Start Something

After a lifetime of endings, after a pattern of partings, after a deluge of dyings, she started simply: starting the car, turning the key, listening for the chunk-a-chunk of some beginning. Then a letter: Dear Joe, Dear Mike, Dear Mom, the complicated art of salutation, knowing how to open, coping with what comes between and before Sincerely, All Best, Faithfully Yours. She practiced opening doors and windows, resisting the urge to close, that surge toward some finish line that she had always seen. She started a job, several jobs, several weeks all focused on orientations, the new employee with packets and forms, all needing filling with that first information, that getting to know you, that setting about, that embarking upon. She launched each day staunchly, deliberately, undertaking a ritual to help her start with the starting, setting the kettle for a fresh pot of tea, and commence the commencing. She started listening, for the perfect way to start conversation, but learned that waving at strangers, just a little, just that small back and forth motion of the hand, palm up and out, fingers slightly bent, was all she could do. To speak first sent her running back into the house, where she started learning a new language, like everyone suggested—Greek, but the only word she could recall was *yassou*, the word for goodbye, so long, talk to you soon. Alice, still clumsy at causing, finally gave in, this initiating too tiring, except when it came to starting a fire: the match strike, the dry wood, the tinder, the surrender of kindling, the conversion of wood into flame, into smoke, all produced by the introduction of one minuscule spark, beginning or ending all one and the same, the transience she knew by its intimate name, the impermanence that burned in her most secret heart.

The Collecting of Fragile Things

requires space, between the curved lash and lens, the quick bend of light, inversion of color and shape, accommodation and suspension, tension—oh the tension—of all that can be captured, seen. I blink as the deer moves into view, a dove-gray twilight strung between us. I watch as she, ballerina, steps through red clover, grass so green it hurts my eyes.

What I know of the vision of deer: it's tied to motion. If I do not move, she cannot see me.

So I step into the grass with her, startling us both into the truth of how we all actually want so much to be seen.

A Poor Girl's History, and Doc Martens

1

I bought mine second-hand, from the thrift shop on the mall called Dapper Dan's. Couldn't afford them new, and I had plans, was gonna spray paint them blue, with swirls, Van Gogh's *Starry Night*, in every step that I made. I bought Cyndi Lauper lace too, tied up my you-can't-be-white hair right there at the counter, as the girl desperately seeking someone didn't even look up as I paid. She did sigh, though, as she counted the coins, tips it had taken me three days waiting tables at The Crow's Nest to make.

2

I wore them with a cute print dress, thick socks, and lace leggings, letting that lace peek between the flounce of the hem and the bite of the boot, like a tease, like a promise, like a threat, like I knew the secret of what it meant to be both wanted and wild.

3

My mama hated them, especially when I wore them with skirts. She scowled, didn't say much, took my fashion defiance, my stomping about in the dirt, with sorrowful silence. I know now this woman who, as a child, had no shoes at all, understood that booted call to power, like we could, both of us, somehow be, in the end, thick-skinned and protected, against the inherited violence of poverty, the legacy of anger and need. Sometimes, it takes a conspiracy to believe.

A Little Blood, A Little Rain

and I am weightless, in orbital perspective, despite how often I pushed too hard, drank too much, smoked and, smoking, layered myself against man after beautiful man—as if he might prove an anchor, a space to be before leaving, stroking the notions of what can be forced and what simply can't. Man after man, I dance, but even in their arms, I am already off, lost in three hundred and sixty-five directions, tossed in my own veins, convinced and convincing myself that the gravity of all of this will, at some point, change.

Shampagne

we swiped from Meeks' Country Store wasn't champagne at all, but white grape juice, Welch's, in a single-serve bottle with a stained label; but out in the mid-seventies dark, running plowed-under tobacco fields, sparklers sputtering in our hands, we pretended, boasted, toasting each other as we passed the bottle between us, dirty-faced dreamers growing wild as the weeds in the trailer park.

Inside the line of single-wides, our folks played hearts and spades, chain-smoked Camels, joked about work or the lack of it, about the money they hadn't made, ate pimiento cheese pinwheels off plastic plates, drank André from Dollar Store tumblers, and ended up dancing in their sock feet on cheap linoleum, clinging to each other, Johnny Mathis singing "Twelfth of Never" to them and to them alone.

They paid us no mind. In the dark, we climbed trees, scrambled up, perched on branches that swung out over the fields. Shampagne made us brave, and we slid farther and farther out on limbs growing thinner and thinner, until we too stood on nothing but dreams, reaching with all we had to where the stars reeled, millions of miles away.

Some Mornings Are Chronic

tenacious in their violence, relentless in the ache that tastes dark as coffee burnt to the bottom of the pot.

I had dreamt of being deaf, of losing the sounds of birds, the wishing whir of water, then worse: in the dream, someone threatened my son, and I, now also mute, found myself incapable of protecting him. I shivered into the kitchen. Arms folded, I stared at things, cups, sink, unable to separate into waking.

It was the morning they blew up Paris.

A hawk, brown as toast, sat at my window. He screeched into the hollow, and then into the wind. His ruff, crowned tuft of white feathers, lifted and fell again and again with each tense high note. Down the road, I could hear the horses, their braying, like wailing, like the barbed wire I always knew would never hold. The hawk screamed for them to stop, but I knew they would run, persistent in their race against this insidious sadness, until their lungs ripped with cold and fire, until their blood left flecked trails on the snow.

Rilke's Sister

Born one year to the day after that first child died, he was dressed
in the little girl's clothes—gowns and lace and buttons laid in chips
of pearl—his sister dead, they put him into the skin she didn't live
long enough in body to wear.

Sometimes he feels her touch him, that curl frizzing at his temple,
straightening the rolled collar, the angle of his hand as he sleeps.
She touches, keeps cool fingertips to his throat, as if to say

Don't trust it, brother, no matter how lonely or sweet it seems.
You are a visitor in this skin, a visitor and dreamer only.

(for Doug Van Gundy)

Any Room Is a Panic Room

if a stranger tries to make small talk with me, Frankie says. She buttons the top two buttons of her best blue coat and looks out the large paned windows of the real estate office where she works doing title searches, days spent alone in deed vaults and hollow courthouse corridors. But now, here, she's inching more and more toward the stone-cobbled street, out to where the wind is so real it seems visible, seen in the racket of leaves, which Frankie says means snow is sure to follow. On the ground a squirrel, fat with winter and ashy gray, runs for cover down a sewer grate. Above the door that Frankie can't wait to push open, low cottony clouds gather, grow heavier and closer, just like Frankie predicted, a landscape of loneliness, as if she'd made it herself, layers of hush and hope, too deep, too deep and too thick not to be believed.

He Wants to Know Why I Move So Fast

Fifth gear, fifth gear, he says, and I'm laughing, already into the next poem, one in which I answer his charge that I move too fast to feel.

Time, I remind him, is not real. Nor is the belief that we have plenty of it.

My mother walked for too long in the has-beens and what-wases, weighed almost to death by regrets, real and imagined. There is no do-over, only begin again. I shed inarticulate skin, some handed to me, some I made myself, and left it all behind me, back there where I hid who I was.

Now, when the sun comes up, I am there ahead to meet it, to grab it with my hands and eat it, to make each fragile moment my own. Let that breaking light pour over and into me, every second of it, nothing missed, until it's shining from every crevice, spilling from every hollow of my naked wanton bones.

The Name Itself

and then the thing, that Wittgensteinian conjecture, the in-between of what we claim and what we think is real. She writes her name on her hand in blue ink, first in English, then in Cherokee signs, unfamiliar to their eyes but speaking what the heart knows. She walks the aisles of her class, hand held forth, palm flat as a plate, offering the strange alphabet to her students, saying

the space between the name and the thing   a shared attempt at making meaning.

More than a thousand languages lost or almost lost already.

Her own movements echo in the classroom after the students leave, as she straightens rows of desks, scuffling chair legs, a move to the right here, a cabinet door closing there.

The silence begs like a thousand forgotten tongues, so she answers, yelling until the sound reverberates from every wall—*I am here. We are all still here.*

I Am Fish and Salt

this woman's flesh; I am hot brine and marsh, foam on rough sand, patches of storm, air warm and tossed and turbulent, wetlands lined with soaking and soaked, this net set and settled, then shredded, ripped to thread and nettle, when the cycles turn. I am forest and shrub, hypoxia and peat. My feet, formed in fire, in lightning strike and coastal burn, reach like estuaries across the bed to where you think you want to lie. My back as deep and black as substrate, my belly-rise like mudflat, I am sawgrass and button bush, sweetleaf and spice, cinnamon fern and ti-ti, swamp rose and dog-hobble. I am cattail, broad and narrow; I am mallow, rose and seashore. I am where everything is born and torn apart. Hear the hearts-a-bursting? I am cottonmouth and otter, heron screech and skunk cabbage, warbler ravaging the armored beetle, damselfly like needles stitching sky to skin. My arms and fingers snake, rake black spike of pine and cypress until they stab into sunlight, clawing night down like the quilt that it is. I am the beginning and the end.

Press your lips into skin and sawgrass, tongue-taste like mineral soil, potassium, nitrogen, phosphorous, foil scratch and metal as blood-letting. I am refuge and I am prospect, holy habitat and loss. I am the forgetting. I am the nursery, the transition, the dead who rise and fall again, the stagnant and the flowing and the slough. I am all there is. I am more than and I am less. I am enough.

I am depository and decomposition, eruption and erosion, of woman born, the start and end of matter. All sticky mud and sea lavender, will you kiss me when I'm brackish? Will you bathe me when I'm fresh?

There Is Someone Asking Not to Be Kissed

or not to be kissed in *that* way any way; or maybe, rather, they're not asking to be kissed, not asking for *that* kind of kiss; rather than asking not, they're not asking, as maybe it's not the kissing, not the kind of kiss, but the asking, the having to ask, the not wanting to ask, the needing to ask, the anticipation of the answer if we do ask or anticipating there that silence with no answer at all, to what we haven't even asked, won't ask, for that kiss, that kind of kiss, the kind that we all know or think we know, that bends us into light, into knowing, into the surrender that goes without asking, that surrender that will free us if only we'd ask, the not asking, that sweet and breathless not asking, that keeps us so so still, closing our eyes so so tight.

The Uncleanness of Women

Blood, they say, is the origin of strife, what keeps me removed, not allowed to touch the husband, nor be wife, not as long as I bleed, nor caress the rough-haired children I bore from that same blood, nor speak their names, nor even make the food that feeds them. I am, they say, defiled, so long now that none can purge it. I free the sacred pigeons from their roost, stroke their peach-spotted wings even while they sing, urge them back into the Lord's own air. No sacrifice is enough; it is no use.

If I give you that coin or two, sewn into my cloak, give it to you for the keeping, will you say—will you only say—that I am healed? In this womanness, sometimes, so much more than blood is lost. Surely, I have learned that there is no love, no love at all, without some cost.

It Is Not What Waits At the Door, This Love

It is not the petals that fall when the roses have given up. It is not the scarred heartwood nor what settles into the trees beneath a calling of stars. It is not the knee bent toward things to be believed in, nor the finger angled toward need. It is not the echoed script the dove leaves on a seamless sky, not the dreamless nights that shiver like sheets on the line, not the *listen listen* of a love song, radio knobs, silver, tuning to voices out beyond the beyond.
It's not the never-be-gone-from-me, not the if-you-leave-I-can't-breathe, not the till-death-do-us-part—no, especially not that—as hearts made of dust already, gold dust, star dust, the dust on the hardwood that, no matter the sweeping it, stays. This love is the always already, the sound that some thousands and thousands of years in the past some heart gasped into being, a whisper, a sentence spoken so softly, and it floats out there beyond everything known, floats toward the no-limits, no limits at all, going on and on and on.

I Will Not Cut Off My Toes for You

like Grimms' Cinderella, but I will carry water in through the green thicket in buckets for us to share. I will cut a branch from the hazelwood tree to sweep our front step while you sharpen your ax and build a sturdy coop with wood and tacks. I will call the white pigeons, and the turtledoves, and promise them straw for their beds in return for the sweetest white pears, the kind you like the best. And I will catch your tears in my hands, then plant them beside my own, surround and protect the saplings with smooth stones I'll fetch from the river's edge until, like us, they grow strong together. And I will brush your hair until you sleep at night, and in the lamplight I will sew us both slippers against the cold floors, and more; I will embroider for you the tiger for strength, the turtle for longevity, on to the sleeves of your coat. I will go with you to the graves of your parents, and I will reach for your hand when I speak the names of my own; and I will dance when you dance, and weep when you weep, and I will give your secrets safekeeping. I will say yes when I mean yes, and no when I mean no, and I will never meet you blind nor expect the same from you. I will meet you strength for strength; I will offer tenderness need to need. No, I will not cut off my toes, nor my heel, nor sit below nor lord above, but I will draw you down into the ashes of who we both have been, who we both have become; I will sweep aside the lentils and peas and relight the fires you think you have lost or forgotten. In among the cinders, I promise that I will love.

Someone Said Once We Are All Deviled

by not knowing how to love. The news recently: a boy, in his twenties, killed on a train trestle in Lynchburg, Virginia, high above the hills painted into fire by November. Declared dead at the scene, he had shoved the girl he held in his arms off the bridge, throwing her into midair flight. She tumbled down toward the broad dark shoulders of the James River, right before the rumble just as he was hit, that last minute gone eternal.

Mama called after me all those years when I walked railroad tracks, attracted to the danger of trestles, testing that devil my own way, even as the whistle warned and warned that I could be torn to pieces.

My want fluttered like flags on my sleeves, my need little stones in my shoes. But she understood that wanting, that want. She told me, once, a story of how, when a child, she had climbed the roof of the shack where they'd lived, and no one had known where she'd gone.

Lost are we in the dark county of the heart, slowing, stopping even, as the train tops the hill, round the bend on one of those rural roads with no lights and no lines. Are we afraid of looking or afraid to find?

I wake up still at night, in a town with no trains, and open the winter window, let the cold seep in, and trace lines like rails on the frost-painted panes.

Deer, Inarticulated

prone, in my drive, already broken out of body when I arrived, but still warm, my palm on his chest. This buck, six points and brawny, I knew best as Wanderer, the fawn I named for his courage, skittering, last spring, from our woods, brazen on his new legs like sticks, even while his twin, the doe, clung to their mother's side in the thick shade of the trees. I'd left them corn, and apples, bits of broccoli he nuzzled up from the grass with his wide black nose, watching me the whole time, bold.

Now, in the cold December dusk, on my knees, I knew him again, but grown, ripe with his buck's musk, but gone, body still but not, not the deer child I'd known but some antlered arrangement, proud head, thick hide, broken free of the frame too fragile, ever too small for both the freedom and the pain to simultaneously fit inside.

I stood, walked the black skid marks on the road, tracked the trail of blood he'd left, gathered up fragments of ripped fur, shards of bone, one piece near the ditch as big as my palm, round as a bowl, the crown of his strong hip a glistening pink hole, ripped, ragged, raw.

I brought it all back to him, made a small pile in the white beams of my headlights, and sat, both of us stranded in that eternal half a mile he'd staggered from being hit to being home.

I had an idea that if I left him, it would be me who was left most alone.

For Dawn and a Dollar

I'd walk the Natchez Trace for you, barefoot and as guileless as a middle-aged widow can be, in that apricot light, in the starting over we're all supposed to chase after, in that keep a dollar in your pocket just in case way that Mama taught me so so many years ago. Tell yourself there ain't no risk, if that's what it takes for you to quit giving in to fear. I'll be your just in case. I'll be your fair to middling. I'll be your hitchhiking shoes, your hot bass blues, your last best chance, your nearly home. 'Cause that's all any of us got, after all, the long-road lope, the fragile hope that we're not walking this road alone.

Instead of Prayer

I will bring you bread. I will bring you beans and blankets. In the blackened pot my mother gave me, I will simmer onion, carrot and heart-shaped cloves of garlic until the smell of the earth surrounds us and we remember our true birth, until we recall the warmth of bodies bent and reborn together near a fire, near a wood of ash and oak. I will bring you loaves soaked in wine, purpled with all I carry with me, in me, in bone, in blood. I will break that bread with my fingers, tear it with my teeth, and offer it, as best I can, into your hands. I will trust that you will think it good, that you will understand, and eat.

Love Is a Ferris Wheel

the gears churning and clanking, the handles for pulling, the eyes like whistles, the fingers like bells, girls lingering in line in their faded soft cotton, the secret looks telling of what's hoped and forgotten, the boys shuffling boot feet, grinning and scooting, giving each other shit for the winks and the smiles, the whispers, the wanting, the lift just like longing, the rise and the rising for what feels like miles, the leaving, the breathless leaving the ground, the heart thump, the heart flare, the not caring what's right or allowed, the sky with no end opening up all around, the slowing, the slipping, the so close to knowing, the sway of the cart and the swing of your feet, the tremble beneath when the ground falls away, the stop at the top and the wanting to stay, there in the colors, so faded by day, but oh love the lights, oh how they shine in that carnival night.

Blood Feud in a Place Called Sometime

where they fought over beans, over beans and bread, over who would be fed, and why, why one and not the other, why the child and not the mother, why the whys turning brother on brother, the hunger drawing bloody lines in the sand, the hands clawing skin man to man, where they shook their fists at the graying sky, and took up muddy shovels and picks and swords and sticks, where they faced off, pacing off to the count of ten, where the how and when rolled their eyes to blood, turned their bones to wood, turned their mouths to mud and their hearts to bread, the bread they wished they had, the need now so bad, being all they knew, the cry for beans that would see them through, the hunger for more that made them run, dropping their sticks, to take up guns, to build up bombs in parking lots, to move from threats to warning shots, warning shots that fell like hail while the women wept and babies wailed, and shouting grew big as their hollow eyes, and the men with the bombs called themselves wise, saying we'll put a stop, an end to all this, the beans are ours, and they flipped the switch, they pressed the button, they exploded the world, the curling blaze, the clouds and haze, the slash and fry, they scorched the earth and seared the sky, incinerating all of it, every bit, they burned the mothers and babies and sisters and brothers, the planet itself cracked and split, an end to the feud, at all costs by all means, boiling it down they showed them good, until nothing stood, not a single thing, between those men and a hill of beans.

Waking Up at the End of the Day

he unzips the pain and pours it into paint tubes, neon cerulean, camel ash gray, nickel and copper and blood red and Day-Glo. It is the anger that's Day-Glo and sudden as storm, the calm of the comb growing teeth, scoring across canvas. Outside the garage there is rain, silver in slivers that prick the sky and glaze the sidewalk slick until the sheen draws him to the door. In his pocket, a clutch of brushes, like fingers he's lost. In his fist, tubes of yellow, cadmium, black, twisted with the writhing of another day when color was fact, the only way he was capable of speaking. His wide thumb, square nail scratches at the labels. The great belly of clouds reach their lowest point of descent and, finally, it pours. So he paints, and paints, sheets of rain translucent, honest as razors, rants of the soul, again and again, circuitry overload, great slashes of color, and spray, purples and greens and shades of blue, oily and candid, that say *This is where despair begins. This is where this aching day will be over.*

(for Andrew Turan)

When the Bears Were Starving in Virginia

I gathered acorns from beneath the great oak outside the house. I crawled about, scratched them into small piles, my fingers clawing at dry grass, at the hard ground, for each round little nut, now so precious, now so scarce. The bears climbed fences, knocked at doors, gaunt in their wanting. The one there on my deck, his eyes like shiny black beads, watched, his head drawn down into the square frame of his shoulders, heavy with weakness, with hunger, even as he lumbered closer, his hide loose, his skin dull gray, my own full belly burning like sin.

Listen.

He spoke the names of the first bears, that oldest clan, the disappeared, the way my grandfather told me over the years, of the Ani-tsa-gu-hi. Our brothers and sisters, led by a boy who chose the wooded path, the joyful beds to be made in moss, the soft skin lost beneath that covering of fur, who moved forever into the twilight trees, singing to those behind, as he now sang to me:

Learn.

I want to feed you, I said, fisting what few acorns I could, fingernails torn and bleeding. He swung his head from side to side.

We all need, he murmured, *so much, your kind and mine. In this poverty where we meet, we are all starved.*

He hunkered over, lay down, bared his belly to me, my own hunger carved there for me to see, saying *Take, take of my flesh, and eat.*

In Preparation for an Elegy

1

He got the news while driving. Snow flying as he drove back from the gym, jacked up and happy, in the way people are happy who don't yet know someone they love has cancer.

2

His father is eighty. A vet who still lifts weights twice a week. His mother, a diminutive woman with a regal back, her beauty barely older than when he brought her home from war, stands at his shoulder, fine black brush lines of Korean script drawing time into her eyes. She is tiger and turtle. He pats her hand, calls her Mama. She stands beside him for the news. She is paper and iron.

3

The son drives eight hours, calling friends from the road, on the way to his parents in Florida. His father is cheery on the phone, despite what they say about his kidneys, his liver. Storm clouds gather over the interstate near Savannah, but they're not gray, they're pink and purple, taking him way back, making him think of an album cover from the '80s. Back then he himself was young and strong. Back then he loved that his father was stronger.

4

Elderly patients with advanced cancer must be allowed to balance the potential risks and benefits of treatment when deciding whether or not to have chemotherapy. The response rates to aggressive chemotherapy are similar in younger and older patients. Disease-related survival is often similar, although the older age group has more deaths due to comorbid illnesses. Factors complicating chemotherapy in the elderly are the physiological changes of aging, the presence of comorbidities and polypharmacy. Organ toxicities may be more problematic in the elderly, but in most tumors, the efficacy of chemotherapy is not age dependent. Chemotherapy, where indicated for advanced cancer, can therefore be safely and effectively used in selected elderly patients.

The abbreviation used by medical professionals for *diagnosis* is *DX*. In military slang, it means *damage exchange,* trading out a damaged item for a new or better one. In internet slang, it represents either someone screaming or a dead man.

5

His father sits in the recliner watching Thanksgiving football. He laughs, a booming sound, and smiles when his mother says, *Mikey, let's go for a walk.* She leads him through the quiet neighborhood, talking about small things, big things, things she's never told him before. She turns her face, like a bird, to check periodically that her son is still there.

He thinks about the bullet-wound scar still puckering on her thin arm. He thinks about his dad as a young soldier dad touching that scar in the cold Korean winter. He thinks that he will have to move furniture to fit in her favorite chair, when the time comes. They turn back toward home, and he hears his father laughing, a drifting sound as distant as the sun.

Winter Is a Wing-Ache

a need a pull a jostle a wish a willingness to sling yourself against the sky sling yourself into the try bring yourself to the edge if it will lead your heart back to warm. It is a stick a silhouette a net made of forgetting and want edging lakes made like mirrors a trick of the memory of heat that keeps slipping away the nearer you come. It is a pan and a bowl and a cup all turned up empty, the sky too empty and weak and sooty as coal and beaten as silver and mocking as the crows who draw back each day with their sharp-tipped beaks. It is the everything we've ever given away. It is a plea a reach a heron scratching at ruin slim-legged stealth gawky and awkward in our own skins and the skins that we make from whatever we find wandering blind in the gray church of a meadow. It is the rhyme we don't want to know the ice tick like clocks the ceiling too low the heron's ascension on wingbeat that repeats *This, this is as far as you go.*

I Will Be Your Country Soon

Pomegranate in my teeth, I will dance like Salome, like Sheba. Shine like seeds sewn into the hem of the robe of ephod for the high priest, etched by Solomon into temple columns, penned into poems for his queen, bent into the fine filigree of his crown, on the first round coins of Judea, for righteousness, one of Deuteronomy's holy seven, maybe, even, some say, our last bite of heaven.

Face smeared with juice, I will return you to abundance, back to the garden, guard your right not to be holy, or even whole. Just be.

The country of you and me. Loneliness and lust, as old a coupling as anything righteous. My body spooned warm against you like the unnamed woman called by incantation by a bearded lonely man in ancient Assyria, with binding spells, hunched over carpets made by other men's wives for sale at market. He paid with fifteen sheaves of barley and a nugget of bronze. His enchantment, if we choose, continues on. We will feed, and be fed, by the magic in those hard seeds, sweet and red, fruit of all longing, as ancient as dust.

When Angels Come in Earthquakes

we can't see them. Well, we can, but what we see is rubble,
or the rubble keeps us from seeing, or the seeing itself is rubble
because our eyes are filled with dust. When angels come in
earthquakes, we rush forward, mistaking them for smoke, or
the smoke that fills our eyes keeps us blinded, keeps us choked,
or they cloak themselves in smoke so that we, in all our blindness,
will not impede them from their missions. When angels come in
earthquakes, in the furor and the fission, we see only fire and
trouble, we see rendering asunder, we see fear and think it's
thunder, we see earth that cracks and crumbles even though
they catch us when we stumble, we see prophecy and doom in
angel skies that burn us blue. When angels come in earthquakes,
we can't see them. Well, we can, but we quake too hard for rescue,
we go racing for redemption, and ascension, for something that
we're hoping, for what we can't see that we need, those roads
on fire a blessing, breaking open finally with some magnitude
of grace.

While Searching This Morning Through Poems About Longing

I came across words for what is untranslatable, the ache that lingers— the German *sensücht*, the Portuguese s*audade,* the Romanian *dor*. In Korean, *keurium,* they speak of reflection and yearning for that which left a deep impression in the heart.

Is it nostalgia then? Or more the search for some far-off country, earthly or not, the wish for some riff, fragmented notes that can neither be forgotten nor retrieved, never gone, this distant sound we have always heard, and recognize, so familiar that we believe enough to call it *home*?

I ran, so hard, my whole life, toward something—a music stand in an empty room, outsized sheet music slightly askew, untouched but waiting. The wooden floors around the stand, striped with sun and shadow, set a stage I saw, again and again, for the singer without a song.

And now you're dead, and I think of how I used to listen, from another room, humming softly to myself, while you played guitar just like loving, and how there is no word for that, how nothing mattered more than simply following along.

My Hips Roll Like Clay

rise like rusted moon, tried and trying, mountain-born woman,
fifty plus years of being pliant, compliant, going and coming,
hard and sturdy, joint and bone generous, rough and ready still,
if needed, as Pap's truck up on its blocks, both of us knowing what
it means to be forever going, forever stopped, overused, overloved.

Hips, lips, hands, my ribs are windows, pelvis doors, giving birth to
my own needs, and yours, and yours, and yours, and his, and hers,
and theirs, seeding, sowing, weeds and blossom given back to the
field, to the holler, to that one folded dollar pinned to cloth and
dress, prayer bound to breast, round to the drive-me-home call
of the folded road at 25, 45, 65 miles per hour, to the fog you can't
resist lifting, to the sin of forgetting what all needs forgiving.

Mother mouth-call and belly, nipples rock hard and tossed with
babies who suck me into, make me geography, topography of
hungry, thighs yawning like valley, like meadow, like river
that you dream of crossing, again and again.

Woman, they all say, *Let me out, let me in.*

Climb me until I'm prime timber hardwood, tend me like kindling,
pull me to you, spilling, buttocks and spine, and make mine all that
hurts or haunts. I am, after all, the vessel that remains. Know me—
all coal shudder and vein and kidney and lung swamp—and want,
so much hunger and so much want.

Trailer Park Oracle

My mama, divining prophecies with playing cards, the same way the Travelers had, a pack of fifty-cent Bicycle cards, and what they used to call *the knack*. The neighbor women they'd knock, carrying pie wrapped in raggedy kitchen cloths, come looking for coffee, they said, you know, just a visit and some and talk. Mama'd slice a piece of whatever they brought along, pour strong black joe into her best chipped mug, while these factory mamas with names like Janine or Doris or Juanita or Flo shushed their wild-eyed kids into silence on my mama's throw rug. *Gonna bet a full house?* she'd ask, like it mattered, for the cards made the call, whether they'd be leaving that day all starry-eyed, the beguiling Two of Hearts leaving them smiling at love coming their way, or crying and baying at the news that their lives were, in fact, even more tattered and sorry than they thought. Hearts for Love and Happiness; Diamonds—Enterprise and Work. Clubs, they meant money, something none of us ever had. Spades, they'd tell trouble, always bad, and hurt. We were all caught in Mama's spell. Four of Spades meant betrayal. Ace of Spades was worse, its curse of death clear in that little black shovel. I stayed near the trailer door, rocking in my run-over shoes, for when the cards made them cry, for when there was bad news, hoping that she'd not tell them, hoping that she'd lie. But Mama called them as they played, no cushioning the blow. She'd light another Tareyton, take another bite of pie, and ask through the haze of light blue smoke, *Better, ain't it, girl? Wouldn't you rather know?*

Hope Is a Folding Chair

the kind we took out into the wide winter field behind Ronald and Julie's South Georgia farm to watch the supermoon rise, a giant red ball at the edge of the sky, just six months before you would die. That night, though, couldn't be about going, but about side by side in those chairs, being still and knowing, that there are things come once in a lifetime. You built a fire on cold sand, then held my hand, grinning, asking, *That big enough sky there for ya, Missy?*

Hope is the coffee you couldn't drink anymore, but still made, poured into a chunky blue mug you knew I loved, and brought to me in bed before I could speak, still caught up in that safe-in-your-arms sleep, warming my day into being with that deep Georgia drawl, teasing with a grin: *You have many gifts, girl—but making coffee is not one of 'em.*

Hope is the curtain hung between us and the mountain at daybreak, summer in Ellijay, drapes you drew back so I could see the sunrise from bed. My head on your chest, your skin Cherokee gold, you crooning "Mary in the Morning" while I listened to your heart play percussion, sweet tenor in flesh-and-bone stereo, until you whispered, *I will never actually leave you, you know.*

Hope is the rug pulled out from beneath us, the great cosmic plan knocking us both off our feet, as your big heart grew weak from the lasting, your smile softly lit—as if you didn't know you were my home in this world—and you kept teasing and asking *Why you always so sweet to me, girl?*

Hope is the lamp I keep lit, even now, having quit asking why or caring how, the light being what matters, in that west-facing window, where sparrows and cardinals play chase and scatter, where pines burn in the sun when it sets, where the moon wanders down every morning, its silver face so much like yearning, like days turning into years, like never, like never forget.

From the Bones of Flowers

Today I'm building myself from the bones of flowers. Mostly the buttercups that persist in the overgrown yard, the lone pink tulip that insists on living, the white-limbed froth of the dogwood tangling its arms around the white pine, and my favorite, stubborn ground gold, the dandelion, its hollow round stem milky with spring.

I am making my own bones of these, replicating, taking forms green and wet, forgetting whatever it is that I'm told to be, whatever had been said, and leaning instead into the dirt, working my way back toward the beginning of all acts of being, back to that sweet dark space just beneath the surface, when the seed knew, at last, its own light, knew the holy work to be done, and set about creating its own delicate limbs and, shining an impossible green, reached for the sun.

200 Miles from Baltimore

the sky is blue and seamless, the hay fields quiet, except for the tumble of my dogs where I walk them toward the woods. There is no evidence here that we are at war.

Back at the house, my twenty-year-old son sleeps after an all-nighter prepping for an exam, his runner's body slung carelessly, free, across his bed, his long-lidded Indian eyes closed, sleep hiding away their light, the bright dreams he keeps there. *He is safe*, I say to myself. I pray for mothers I don't know, for mothers losing sons everywhere.

My Husky mutt chases a starling, oblivious to everything but her own joy. Big Zeke, with his black Boxer's body and soulful Lab eyes, stays close, at my hip, trusting that I'll keep him safe out here in the world, safe and whole until we arrive home. I kneel, hug him hard, feeling even in his big chest the quicksilver fragility of his bones.

Twice a Day, the Tide Erases

the palette beneath that peach sky, that Gulf Coast sun, clearing the way for the manta rays, their triangular wings ghosting just beneath the inky water. In Jamaica, they call them devilfish; in Queensland, angels of the ocean. Here, they are dancers, performing just for the old man who fishes from the pier every day, every year, since the work ended. He leans in, reads the waves, sand bars bending like hieroglyphs, like handwriting, watches the seldom tourists who stumble into his little corner of prayer. Today a father is there, two near-grown daughters, cameras in hand. The father in a ball cap nods. The youngest girl speaks, the older smiles into the sun as it melts across the sky. Below them, a manta spins and circles, making a map for this quiet meeting of hearts, a map to where the world starts. Above them, a scatter of seabirds. In the faraway city the birds mimic the sound of subway cars, metal on metal. Here, they compete on the wind to capture the sound of girls laughing below, lit by that burning sun; of their father calling the words he would leave them —*Love*—*Believe*—after them as they run.

(for Jerry Mathes)

What I Will Give You, If You Will Let Me

The word *Free*, freely given, as it was meant to be, from the Gothic *freis*; from Proto-Indo-European *prijos*, dear; from the root in Sanskrit *pri-*, to love, *priyah*, my friend, my own, beloved. The word *Friend* rises there, too, from Proto-Germanic *frijand*, Old Norse *frændi*, Old Frisian *friund*; also *Wife*, from the Old English *freo* for wife, or Old Norse *Frigg*, she who was wife of Odin, or the Middle Low German *vrien*, to take to wife; and *Peace*, from the Gothic and Old English *friðu*.

Free, and *Friend*, and *Peace*.

If we are to fall in love, all of us, this, it seems, would be the place to start.

How to Fry Catfish

Dredged it in eggs, milk, Worcestershire, all whisked to a high froth, cornmeal and flour, tossed and sifted together by hands that know what it means to give. Filets or in strips made from cuts along the natural seams, flesh fed on the lowland movement of water, the slow hot crawl of sun on sand. Batter by hand, fingers gloved in that floury mix, rolled and salted, peppered down, secretly spiced. The oil matters—peanut oil—the consistent boil in that cast iron pan just right, filets curling as they fry, the slow slide from brown to gold, all crisp and crunch and hot bite, that earth feed and dance of skin, that thing we crave—sustenance.

Remember:

When they surrender, they bring their voices with them, that mournful sound, swamp song at dusk, big cats old men hoist up from the dark water: blues, yellows, channel cats, flathead. Those men, their own voices marshy with age, shouldered in among the sage beguile of cattails, scold in low tones: *Gut 'em quick. Keep 'em iced. Fry 'em right.*

The way you handle anything at its end means something. Put them in good company, slaw and hushpuppies, tea sweet and dark and dense as the water where, when you least expected it, they gave themselves up, gave their last breath to your hands, singing.

The Universe in Three Acts: Please Refer to Your Handout

Even the Bible, he said, begins in STASIS, the world, this world, all worlds, the original swirl of encompassing darkness, entropy blanketing entropy, unfolding, folding in and over itself—endlessly.

INTRUSION: Action into stasis, some ripple, some beginning, of limitation or shape, that one corner taking charge of the fold, making into itself, running into becoming—visible, viable, real.

Is it possible for that which creates to intrude upon itself?

CONFLICT, he said, is created by intrusion plus desire. The ghost and its shadow, evolving at the edge of belief, like so much cosmic swamp grass, sharp little blades, maybe green, curving blade into blade into rib and stone, alone and crawling, up on the shore of a story.

Let there be.

And it was good.

Until we step in front of ourselves, OBSTACLE thrumming with that same desire that made us, self-made marathon of sins, like picking clothes from a rack, or skins, fingering through until we are forced to choose an ACTION.

Resolution? No caps. No pause. Some stone tablets, maybe, that say —in the end of the beginning of the end—This is your mess after all. You made it. It is now yours to RESOLVE.

(for Richard Schmitt)

A Chant Against Lonely

One focus point in the brain, one lobe, one light, sitting up on the side of the bed at night, fingers tapping out incantations in the rumpled sheets, some sleep-deprived meditation.

Say *I am open.* Say *I am willing.* Say *I am hungry.* Say *I am ready,* even if you're not.

The bed is hot and empty; the windows ache toward a deep night sky now too familiar. Constellation identification, even as the seasons reel. How the deer drift, take their time, no need to run this late, in the winter hay field. How the trees, so upright in daylight, lean toward the road when no one is watching. But you're watching.

Say *This is what I remember.* Say *This is what I have learned.* Say *This is what I deserve.*

You trace Orion one star at a time across the empty side of the bed, again and again. Consistency, you're told, is key. So you repeat some mantra you think you're making, until it all just becomes shaking in theories of time and space.

Say *This is where I will show you the night sky.* Say *This is where the lonely come to die.* Say *This is all I know, but I will share it with you.*

You say and say, wait for light to remake the day, for the blueing start of dawn, when you rise and, once again, move on.

Say *There is a magnet dislocated in my heart.* Say *The windows are inked like an atlas.* Say *I am no better than geese, calling calling, searching and bent, on someplace like home.*

If I Am to Die by Fire

let it be pentecostal, let it be redemptive, let it be like atonement, falling and preemptive like flame from the sky. Let it be meteoric, let it slash sideways like the worst of rains, let it burst from the heavens like a river of lava, let it drip from the hands of the gods, turning the sky into an unrelenting ocean, into a cathedral of noise, a torrent of sound; let it burn, let it sear, let me hear and feel the surrender of flesh, of meat into smoke, as it reinvents pain into release, into joy.

Signs of Winter Mammals

Young trees with bark rubbed off, a buck shining his antlers. Or deeper, scratched, the bear roused from her torpor just long enough for a forage into the winter garden, for snow-covered cabbage, for the lush reach of kale, broad paw prints leading back to the den she has built into the convenience of roots in a fallen great oak.

Meandering impressions, runways through a field of yellow grass made by small rodents, the white-footed mouse, the short-tailed shrew. The wander of the fisher cat, maybe even a mink, a snag rumbled open where they searched for food.

Holes in dead wood, dug into for hibernation, lined with straw and leaves. Pine cones picked clean of seed. Black walnuts cracked in half, a scatter of tiny bowls left behind among the quick light tracks of the fox. Young trees and shrubs, bases girdled, stripped of tender bark, by rabbits, hares, and voles at or above the snow line. Raccoon tracks, like the smallest of hands, on the crust before the sun melts it.

Tufts of fur like little flags on low-hanging limbs, caught as they make their way in and out in the dark. Those hard hickory nuts, nibbled on the edges by fat gray squirrels who escape above to a large leafy nest in the bare gray branches. The rare sighting of the shy possum on a day feed. The persistent smell of skunk on the clean winter wind.

Scat of all kinds, and the tracks—deer, coyote, coywolf—often leading to the pond's edge where they've fed on the hardy scrub left behind from the trees brought down by the beaver. The beavers themselves, families blended together in one large lodge for comfort, for warmth.

The woman, wandering there too, burrowed into her own coat and scarf, steeled against the chill, where she stops at a scattered circle of feathers and bone, all that remains of some predator's meal. Mammal too, her belly tugs with winter hunger, as she thinks of how badly she sometimes wants to den in, disappear into and sleep, invisible there, deep beneath the frozen ribs of this winter's hill.

Last Night I Prayed for Rain

solstice moon rising early, joining me to wait for the short night, long sun. Last night I prayed for love, for what there is to be won in the soaking, the drenching, the washing away. Last night I prayed to be empty, to be full. The moon fell behind clouds, behind my wanting, but not before dropping silver coins into my upraised hands, not before the flowers around me, turned to say my name in their silver voices, to say *You are empty, you are full, you are empty, you are full,* just before the lightning started, just before the storm came.

*You Need to Know Something Else
About This Softness*

that I have been looking for you, traveling from place to
place, a circuit, moving as the way, not the means. A life made
of in between—preacher, judge, farmhand—or the peddler, a
selling of moment to moment, in the territories of carnivorous
want, haunting a dark wood working, and wandering, houses like
dreams where no one lives, along stretches of field, brown dirt and
the curve of gravel roads. I thought, once, I'd found you in a stand
of alder and oak, on a mountain where clouds were close as skin.
But that wasn't it, wasn't you, just smoke on the hills from the fire
I'd lit. How is it that we squander comfort so willingly? And I am,
I guess, off again, on a lane with few patches of light, suspended
between tenses—what was, what can be—delicious contingency,
satchel and blanket and bread, the now and again beds of a life
itinerantly tender.

The Language of Ice

says *I will not miss you.* It curls around the yellowed stem of the marsh grass, whispering Ecclesiastes—*Is there any thing whereof it may be said, See, this is new? It hath been already of old time, which was before us.* The grass, too, does not long for us, its song even now surrendering to the cold clasp of December. Wintered in, the pond shivers beneath a translucent crust, oak leaves held in place, silvered in their going. *The thing that hath been, it is that which shall be; and that which is done is that which shall be done.* This ice, this grass, the stones here beneath my boot, the deer who use their hooves to break the frozen surface across the way, their long tongues playing at, tugging up the coontail, the pondweed, all say *We will not miss you.* The sun splinters bare trees into matchsticks, into tinder, persistent silhouettes against wide and endless blue. Above, a heron flies past, great sweeps of wing. He tells stories of last year's cold, of the knowing that keeps him from loving us in the way that we want.

On the Darkening Green

spring wet and new, the lights come, first one, then two, then
too many to number, fireflies rising from their day of sleep in
those beetled catacombs beneath dark earth, as if they're made,
themselves, of death and birth. *Photinus brimleyi.* Slow signal,
a series of short flashes of yellow, intervals ten seconds long,
bioluminescent love songs leaving echoes like powder on the
storm-washed air. *I need,* he says, *I want.*

The female, wingless, dreams the forest floor into being, turning
dirt, leaf, the lost hold of moss, a slow shelf of roots, until seeing
him, finally, like a moon she's dreamt up, like the sky itself finally
clear, she flashes—only once—that singular response as bright
as it is rare, that whisper as night settles, the voice that says
I'm here, and I care.

(after the painting by Jonathan Kevin Rice)

Instead of Wings

I've broken bones, shoulder blades that fold like paper clips, ribs stretched and cracked from carrying babies, three of them pressed into the spiny cage of my back, tumbling down through the dark passage between my hips. Femur song, long bones hollow now as flutes. Maybe that's the sound you hear when you sink down into me, wind singing through empty space, a woman's history of giving as displaced as stars in that vast and distant sky. Sometimes when I come, I cry from the beautiful collapse and explosion, from the tender notion that all women have harbored over time—that maybe you can still teach me how to fly.

Not the Bloom

or blossom with its folded wing, the grazing voice, the footstep
left in sodden sand, the lover, child, or mother, no longer there,
even our own skin, where we think we live, all fragrant bone and
snapped sinew. Gone. Let the swamp take what it will, the stillness,
the slide on into true, the not held and never known, the not ever
us. Let's not mourn what isn't ours and never was.

Praise This and That

no matter the slip of time, no matter the hip that aches at night,
no matter the growing silence that stands at the edge of the bed,
waiting for you to rise into another day past fifty, another year past
young. Praise the getting up, praise the shower songs to be sung.
Praise the towel, the soap, the float of lavender-scented steam.
Praise the lingering edges of a dream you want to remember,
and then praise the memory as it slides away. Praise the click and
hum of the heater as it warms the day. Praise the robe like a frayed
old friend. Praise the beginning of the day and the reminder that
night can end. Praise the miracle of pockets, the clink of the chain
and locket you string around your neck. Praise the giggle that
comes when you're glad that no one hears you sing in the morning.
Praise the desire that keeps you singing. Praise the foggy mirror,
the sweetness of toothpaste, the ringing clink of cups on counters.
Praise the shuffle-comfort of slippers, praise the arch of the foot
and the more than half a century of walking. Praise the coolness
of the tile, the remembered talk of children and their school-
day laughter. Especially praise the tender mothering of water.
Praise the doors and windows, that they open and close as they do.
Praise the light switch and the fragile bulb, the pup who shakes
with joy that you're awake. Praise the give and the take of family.
Praise even that angry cat with her yellow eyes who waits in the
middle of the kitchen floor, looking pointedly at the door while the
coffee brews, who points her lock-picking paw at you as if to say,
You are not, you know, as quick as you used to be. Praise the brown-
edged toast, the seaside smell of butter as it melts, the cream that
ribbons the coffee, the svelte red bird with its glass-bead eye who
watches you through the window that needs washing, wanting
to know exactly when you plan to put out that seed you promised.
Praise the music of his scolding, the way he ignores the caucusing
crows. Praise the clothes, both clean and in need of washing.

Praise the sweater your mother gave you, the one you thought
you hated but know now feels like love. Praise the practicality
of closets, the keys that jingle as you claim them. Praise the rituals
as you name them. Praise the doorway where you linger, to look
back at the tumble of sheets you're grateful to have but haven't
straightened. Praise the way your throat thickens, the elevator
drop of your heart; praise the tears of remembering when.
Praise all things, the beginning and the end. Praise the struggle
and the storm and the sun that follows, that ladder of light from
window to floor. Praise the constancy of both the living and
the dead. Praise knowing how to live and learning how to die.
Praise even the cold side of the bed, where love used to lie.
Praise the door as you close it. Praise the gratitude you feel
for the warmth, for the loss, but especially for the love,
for having had the chance, if even for a time, to know it.

Notions of the Body

> *Architecture is a reflection or a substitution for the self, a surrogate body.*
>
> —Anish Kapoor

That song we learned as kids—head and shoulders, knees and toes—sometimes she sings it, walking down the sidewalk toward work, toward rooms filled with bodies, and being, toward the creation of a common world made in tandem, in agreement, the shared perceptions we create on that sidewalk, in that classroom, in line at the bank.

She had bitten back the urge to hum it, that song, throat thick, inappropriate and ineffective surge of memory, while bathing her near-to-dying mother in those last few days, cleaning skin like paperwhites, the fragile touch of time weighing in the long sway of her eighty-year-old breasts. They both winced at the institutional roughness of the hospital bath cloth dragging wet lines along the brittle bony intersections of her fine wrists and spine.

Her mother had cried, her small back bent, shoulders folded like wings. Together on their knees, wet hospital tile, they spoke of the fading, the going and the staying, the illusion of seeing, the making of each other, the being by what is perceived.

Now, her mother gone, when she feels most alone, she kneels like that again, washes her own aging skin, intentional moving within, hoping for her mother's grace in the face of this body giving in.

Is it true, then, that it is what we make it?

Sometimes, like a body within a body, she feels more—and more, and then some—beyond what one suit of skin, no matter how luminous, can long store, like nesting dolls. The dissolution of this notion of flesh as rigid; instead, the body itself becomes ambiguous. *I. You. Us.*

Then there's the lover's hand, and the notion of flesh bursts any idea of subjectivity, bringing to light the reciprocity, the interlacing of the body and the world. *C'mere, girl.* Hands on her belly, face, arm, she knows herself as less a thing, an object—*I have a body*—and more a subject—*I am a body. Head and shoulders, knees and toes, knees and toes. I am this. I am this. I am so much more.*

Grace Where You Find It

> *And there was no dance, / no holy place*
> *from which we were absent.*
>
> —Sappho

Talk me down, if you can. There is so much to be dangerous about. That knowing that has shimmered just beyond me as long as I remember, disarticulated light, shivers of what can be like streetlight glimmers on a hotel window. Below, by the pool, by all the pools, beautiful young men with dark trimmed beards and young women with boys' hips and year-round tans who smiled without moving their mouths—it seemed they all knew.

I saved my tips from the bar to pay for a night at the 6 just so I could watch TV in color. If the bikers at the Swinging Curve tipped well, I stayed two nights—one to watch Bobby on *Dallas*, the extra to work up my nerve. Even then, I was looking for you.

I didn't know the rules. In this hand a Bible, in that one a knife. The man I saw die, OD just feet away from me, when I was fourteen changed everything, my drug dealer boyfriend hushing me up, rushing me out, into a night too poor even for stars.

Mama said find someone stronger than you are. It happened once, but he died.

And now I fumble again, hands smelling like metal, like blood, like love when it knows that it's leaving. Mama was right. It didn't come easy.

I understood it back then, back when the rules were about spare change and flat tires and making it until payday, when the space and ways of being alone were so commonplace I didn't even know I was lonely. But that was before the game rearranged, before learning how *desire*, said soft and true, sounds just like *danger*.

A long way from the bar, all respectable now, I'm not sure how, but MasterCard pays for the room—somewhere, anywhere, as long as I can drive there—a Hilton in Manhattan, a Ramada in Georgia, with its kerosene coffee and breakfast bar crowded with kids with bare feet and parents who could care less about cost in that vacation moment. I move among them, still the poor girl on fire, dancing with loss.

And their knowing still shimmers, white crescents of light like chance on the surface of the pool, in the frosted light fixtures glowing hard in hallways that smell like chlorine. The voices of families follow me. They know what they mean, what they've got, and what they need. They talk about what they deserve.

I don't even know what I've learned. In some of the cities I drive to, shots are fired. Someone dashes to the metro, afraid they'll miss the last train. Someone else, maybe lovers, walk instead in the rain, because they're in love and so lovely. In a hotel room somewhere, they'll watch movies in black and white, on purpose, and find it charming, subtitles disarming them as they drift off and dream.

I know someday, outside Macon, I'll leave the pony-tailed girl who brings my one cup of coffee a twenty-dollar tip, won't wait to see her look up in surprise or slip it into the apron tied round her hips, won't wait to see if she even looks out to see the woman leaving, always leaving, outside, holding sandals in her hand, jumping into a bright red car. Talk me down, if you can.
But I still have so far to drive.

Acknowledgments

Some of the poems here were originally published in the following journals. Thanks to these editors for their encouragement and for their continuing efforts toward the beautiful work, the good and too often thankless work, for literature and art and heart that so benefits us all.

Blue Heron Review: "It Is Not What Waits At the Door, This Love"
Bridge Eight: "Alice Learns to Start Something"
Consequence Magazine: "Last Night I Prayed for Rain," "The Universe in Three Acts: Please Refer to Your Handout"
Cultural Weekly: "A Poor Girl's History, and Doc Martens," "Some Mornings Are Chronic," "Instead of Wings"
Dove Tales: "Deer Inarticulated," "Notions of the Body," "200 Miles From Baltimore"
Iodine Poetry Journal: "On the Darkening Green"
Journal of Compressed Creative Arts: "Not the Bloom"
Spank the Carp: "Love Is a Ferris Wheel," "Blood Feud In a Place Called Sometime"
Tar River Poetry: "The Bones of Flowers"
Third Wednesday: "In Preparation for An Elegy"
Two Cities Review: "A Chant Against Lonely"
Two Hawks Quarterly: "Shampagne," "Grace Where You Find It"

Cover artwork, "Red Sky" by Desmond Kavanagh; cover and interior book design by Diane Kistner; Droid Serif text and titling

About FutureCycle Press

FutureCycle Press is dedicated to publishing lasting English-language poetry books, chapbooks, and anthologies in both print-on-demand and Kindle ebook formats. Founded in 2007 by long-time independent editor/publishers and partners Diane Kistner and Robert S. King, the press incorporated as a nonprofit in 2012. A number of our editors are distinguished poets and writers in their own right, and we have been actively involved in the small press movement going back to the early seventies.

The FutureCycle Poetry Book Prize and honorarium is awarded annually for the best full-length volume of poetry we publish in a calendar year. Introduced in 2013, our Good Works projects are anthologies devoted to issues of universal significance, with all proceeds donated to a related worthy cause. Our Selected Poems series highlights contemporary poets with a substantial body of work to their credit; with this series we strive to resurrect work that has had limited distribution and is now out of print.

We are dedicated to giving all of the authors we publish the care their work deserves, making our catalog of titles the most diverse and distinguished it can be, and paying forward any earnings to fund more great books.

We've learned a few things about independent publishing over the years. We've also evolved a unique, resilient publishing model that allows us to focus mainly on vetting and preserving for posterity poetry collections of exceptional quality without becoming overwhelmed with bookkeeping and mailing, fundraising activities, or taxing editorial and production "bubbles." To find out more about what we are doing, come see us at www.futurecycle.org.

The FutureCycle Poetry Book Prize

All full-length volumes of poetry published by FutureCycle Press in a given calendar year are considered for the annual FutureCycle Poetry Book Prize. This allows us to consider each submission on its own merits, outside of the context of a contest. Too, the judges see the finished book, which will have benefitted from the beautiful book design and strong editorial gloss we are famous for.

    The book ranked the best in judging is announced as the prize-winner in the subsequent year. There is no fixed monetary award; instead, the winning poet receives an honorarium of 20% of the total net royalties from all poetry books and chapbooks the press sold online in the year the winning book was published. The winner is also accorded the honor of being on the panel of judges for the next year's competition; all judges receive copies of all contending books to keep for their personal library.

www.ingramcontent.com/pod-product-compliance
Lightning Source LLC
LaVergne TN
LVHW020939090426
835512LV00020B/3426